A Guide To Alimony In New Jersey

2nd Edition

Bari Zell Weinberger, Esq.

FAMILY LAW REFERENCE COLLECTION
Weinberger Divorce & Family Law Group

Weinberger Law Group Library
119 Cherry Hill Road, Suite 120
Parsippany, NJ 07054

www.WeinbergerLawGroup.com

ISBN-13: 978-1-942725-22-0

A Guide To Alimony In New Jersey

Table of Contents

About The Author

Bari Z. Weinberger, Esq. is a certified matrimonial law attorney and founding partner of Weinberger Divorce & Family Law Group of New Jersey. Ms. Weinberger has been named a Top Women in Law by New Jersey Law Journal and carries an AV Preeminent (highest) peer rating from Martindale Hubbell. She recently celebrated 10 years of recognition on the state's SuperLawyers list.

In addition to working with clients at her firm, Weinberger Divorce & Family Law Group, Ms. Weinberger is the Associate Author of the New Jersey Family Law Practice, 15th Ed., a 5-volume treatise utilized by virtually every family law judge and practitioner in the State of New Jersey.

www.WeinbergerLawGroup.com

Disclaimer

This book provides a general overview of New Jersey spousal support for informational purposes only. The contents included do not in any way supplement or replace legal advice obtained by a qualified and licensed attorney.

The information provided herein is based solely upon my professional experiences in the areas of New Jersey divorce and family law. While every effort has been made to ensure that the information contained in this book is helpful and of high quality, no representations or warranties of any kind are made with regard to the completeness or accuracy of the included content.

Please note that information provided within this guide is current as of publication date. Due to the complexity and frequency with which the divorce and family laws change, you should consult with a qualified attorney to determine the best course of action for your specific legal needs.

If you require legal advice based on the specifics of your case as it relates to New Jersey laws, please feel free to reach out to our office to schedule a consultation with one of our experienced attorneys. It would be our pleasure to help you.

For more information about other topics related to family law, such as divorce, domestic violence, prenuptial agreements, family mediation, child support and child custody, domestic partnerships, or any other family law related topics, please ask us about our other books. All guides in the series are designed, like this one, to help you to make sound decisions regarding your family's individual situation. Please keep in mind, however, that these books contain general information, and not legal advice. Always direct specific questions about your own situation to an attorney.

Weinberger Divorce & Family Law Group

Safeguarding Your Future™

Letter from the Author

Whether you are the spouse who may need to pay alimony, or the spouse who receives support, I am so glad that you have found your way to this guide. For anyone going through divorce, I advocate learning all you can about your options, especially when it comes to your finances and securing your financial future. As it can play such a critical role in post-divorce finances, alimony is definitely on my recommended list of need-to-know topics.

Only a few decades ago, awarding alimony was a very cut-and-dry decision in most divorces involving long-term marriages. As a result of New Jersey alimony reform laws enacted in 2014, however, times have changed, and along with them, so have alimony options. Today, New Jersey offers five different types of alimony, including limited duration, open durational (formerly known as "permanent alimony"), rehabilitative, reimbursement alimony, and *pendente lite* (temporary) alimony. Which one is most appropriate for your situation? We describe each in the following pages, so please take a look.

Alimony can be a powerful tool to ensure that both spouses are able to enjoy the same standard of living after their divorce as they did during their marriage. Are you the higher earning spouse who has been ordered to pay support? I encourage you to learn all your options for negotiating a fair amount, as well as the tax implications and decisions about assets that may help improve your bottom line. Are you the spouse who will receive support? I urge you to carefully consider what kinds of resources you will need in order to make your lifestyle secure.

This guide provides to you useful information about the actual statutory factors used in determining alimony, what to expect, examples from both sides of the alimony equations, important money-saving tips, and understandable explanations of current alimony laws in New Jersey. Our sincerest hope is for this guide to empower you and help you feel more in control of your finances. However, please note that this book does not replace personal legal advice or legal representation.

I also want to let you know that in matters of money, your welfare, and your future, I feel strongly that the stakes are just too high to have anyone but a qualified, experienced family law attorney by your side. If you are filing for divorce in New Jersey or seeking to modify your current spousal support situation, or if you have questions after reading this guide, please don't hesitate to give us a call. Whenever you need us, our attorneys are here to help.

All my best,

Bari Z. Weinberger

Chapter 1

The History and Purpose of Alimony

Alimony (also called "spousal support" or "spousal maintenance") is an amount of money one spouse pays to the other during divorce proceedings or after a final judgment of divorce.

Traditional and Modern Concepts of Alimony

Alimony is an old concept with roots in the traditional model of marriage that divided responsibilities rigidly according to gender: The husband worked outside of the home and the wife kept the house and cared for the children. Marriage was a lifelong commitment; divorce was available only when one spouse behaved in a way that was clearly harmful to the other spouse. Since women had few opportunities to earn an independent income outside of marriage, when a husband abandoned a wife or was otherwise at fault in ending a marriage, he continued to be responsible for supporting her for the rest of her life.

Marriage has changed in many ways in recent decades. Job and career opportunities for women have grown tremendously, and in the majority of marriages both spouses now work outside of the home. Husbands participate in sharing housework and childcare to a greater degree than ever before.

Factors such as increased economic freedoms, longer lifespans, and a lessening of the social stigma once associated with divorce have led many more couples to choose to end marriages after varying lengths of time. The popularity of fault-based divorce has diminished radically as it has become more and more apparent that court cases involving proof of fault between separating spouses tend to be damaging and draining both financially and emotionally, not only for the separating couple but also for any children the couple might have.

There is a new view of marriage as a partnership that can be dissolved without fault by either party at any time, provided that the spouse who chooses to dissolve it gives proper notice to the other partner and participates in a fair division of the fruits of the partnership. The evolution of "no fault" divorce has followed this new view. The concept of alimony has been evolving rapidly along similar lines.

Accompanying the new view of marriage as a soluble partnership is an increased emphasis in the courts on requiring each spouse to become self-sufficient after marriage, so that each can move on and build a separate life free of encumbrances related to the marriage. This new emphasis is tempered with the recognition that marriage differs from a business partnership in some important respects, not the least of which is that both spouses still enter marriage believing that the commitment will be lifelong. From the very beginning of a marriage, spouses begin to make choices that may work well for the marital partnership, but can pose challenges for the individual if and when the marriage comes to an end.

While strict division of labor along gender lines is now the exception rather than the rule, couples in the majority of marriages still divide roles to some degree. One partner is often a higher earner. One spouse may dedicate more time to developing a career while the other spends more time caring for the home and children. Although both spouses will inevitably experience economic repercussions from the need to create two households out of one during and after a divorce, the impact tends to fall harder on a spouse who has always earned a lower income, or who has spent more time as a homemaker, resulting in an economic dependency on the other spouse. Alimony is a way of evening out this disparity. Courts order alimony when appropriate to acknowledge the joint efforts of a couple in building a standard of living during marriage and to facilitate the ability of both spouses to maintain that standard of living to the greatest extent possible after the marriage.

"Alimony is an amount of money one spouse pays to the other during divorce proceedings or after a final judgment of divorce."

Bari Z. Weinberger, Esq.

Relationship between Alimony and Equitable Distribution of Property

Although an alimony determination is separate from a property distribution and has a different purpose, a court will consider many of the same factors during the two processes. The purpose of property distribution is to divide the assets and liabilities the couple has accumulated during marriage. Alimony, on the other hand, is geared toward protecting one spouse from experiencing disparate economic hardship going forward as a result of the divorce; it is directly related to one party's need for financial support and the other party's ability to pay such support. In spite of these separate purposes, the distribution of property can have an impact on either spouse's need for alimony, while the payment or receipt of alimony can also have an impact on what will be fair in terms of property division.

The interplay between property distribution and alimony can be more pronounced in states like New Jersey where marital property is divided "equitably" (meaning fairly) rather than exactly equally, as it is in community property states like California or Nevada. In some cases, an unequal distribution of property can be useful in eliminating or reducing the necessity for one spouse to assume the ongoing responsibility of alimony payments. Granting a dependent spouse a greater share of property in lieu of alimony can facilitate an earlier and more complete separation of the two spouse's lives. Courts usually consider this kind of earlier and more complete separation to be positive for both former spouses, as it reduces the potential for ongoing financial and emotional entanglement between them after the divorce has been finalized. In some cases, however, a couple may have enjoyed a relatively high standard of living during the marriage due to one spouse's income, but did not accumulate sufficient assets to compensate a dependent spouse through the equitable property distribution. Alimony will then be the only way to prevent the divorce from having a devastating financial impact on that spouse.

For all of these reasons, courts generally consider property distribution and alimony together, and couples attempting to create their own settlement agreements should be aware of the impact that either might have on the other. In considering how the two might work together, certain differences must be kept in mind. For example, an equitable distribution of property is not generally modifiable, while an alimony award can often be modified after the divorce if circumstances substantially change. The two types of awards may have different tax implications. As we will discuss in detail, tax treatment of alimony changed dramatically in 2019, so the tax treatment of new awards will be different than the tax treatment of awards that already existed before the changes went into effect. To some extent, alimony payments and property distributions will also have different implications for purposes of bankruptcy filings.

If you and your spouse are attempting to work out your own marital settlement agreement, you should be careful to distinguish clearly between property distribution and alimony to prevent any misunderstandings down the road. Be certain that you both understand the distinctions and consult with attorneys and financial professionals as needed to ensure this. For more information about the equitable distribution of property in a New Jersey divorce, see our companion e-book in this series, "A Guide To Property Division in New Jersey."

Practical Tip: Beginning in 2019, neither alimony payments nor property distributions are taxable in divorce.

Before 2019, parties designating any large amount of money as a "lump sum alimony payment" risked losing favorable tax treatment by the IRS. Alimony payments, but not property distributions, were considered to be income for the recipient spouse and deductible by the paying spouse. The IRS would generally treat large lump sum payments as property, regardless of what the parties called the payment. For new orders and agreements beginning in 2019, however, there is no longer any tax benefit to lose, as the IRS has discontinued its favorable treatment of alimony payments. Nevertheless, certain property transfers (such as real estate) may create tax implications for the party who wishes to sell the property at a later date. Make sure to consult with your accountant to evaluate the best way to balance the tax effects on both parties of all payments and property distributions.

Relationship between Alimony and Child Support

Unlike alimony, child support in New Jersey is controlled by a very specific calculation of each parent's income and the amount of time a child spends with each parent. For parents with orders of agreements predating 2019, alimony is deducted from the income of the paying parent and included in the income of the receiving parent before child support is calculated. Parties who finalized their alimony agreements by the end of 2018 will continue to follow these rules. For orders and agreements dated 2019 or later, however, the tax treatment of alimony and child support will no longer differ.

Because alimony and child support were formerly subject to different tax treatments, parents attempting to reach agreement on an appropriate amount of alimony would consider the impact of child support calculations as part of an alimony negotiation. A parent in a high-income bracket was sometimes able to pay a slightly higher amount in alimony without a proportional financial impact, because paying tax deductible alimony might decrease the amount of child support the parent was required to pay. If the spouse receiving alimony was in a lower tax bracket, the tax effect of receiving more taxable alimony as opposed to non-taxable child support might be minimal. In some cases, changing the payment structure slightly could actually result in a net gain for both parties. With the new tax treatment of alimony, this kind of calculation is no longer relevant. Alimony and child support should still be considered together, as the total amount of resources available to a household will depend on both of these items, but their tax treatment will no longer differ.

Alimony Reforms of 2014

On September 10, 2014, Governor Chris Christie signed into law a comprehensive alimony reform bill designed to reflect recent social changes and bring greater fairness to New Jersey alimony law. For the most part, the reformed statute applies only to alimony orders and agreements put into place after the reform laws were passed. The changes mainly affect the following:

- **Permanent Alimony has been Replaced with Open Durational Alimony**: In addition to changing the name of alimony payments without a pre-determined expiration date from "permanent" to "open durational," the statute limits this kind of alimony award to marriages of 20 years or longer, absent exceptional circumstances.

- **Duration of Other Types of Alimony**: When a marriage lasts fewer than 20 years, the duration of alimony payments can no longer exceed the length of the marriage unless a judge decides there are "exceptional circumstances."

- **Cohabitation after Divorce:** Judges can now to suspend or end payments if the recipient enters into a marriage-like relationship with a partner, even if they do not get married, and sometimes even if they are not living together full-time.

- **Income/Job Changes:** Judges will be able to lower payments for payers who have been out of work for 90 days.

You can find more information on the 2014 reforms throughout this book. If you have an alimony order or agreement that predates the revisions (anytime prior to September 10, 2014), there are some circumstances in which courts will analyze requests for modification or termination of your payments differently than requests for modification or termination of orders or agreements implemented under the revised statute. This accommodates the expectations of parties bound by those earlier orders or agreements that any requests for modification or termination would be determined by currently existing law. For this reason, as well as for the purpose of providing a broad context, in this e-book we will discuss the law as it existed prior to the recent reforms as well as the current law.

Alimony Tax Treatment Before and After 2019

This following example shows how the 2019 revisions to the federal tax code could affect both the amount of alimony one party receives and the amount of money available as a whole to a divorced couple. The example is very detailed, but worth following through if you want to really understand the full implications of the changes:

Dylan and Casey

Dylan earns $300,000 per year and Casey earns $80,000. Under their marital settlement agreement, Dylan pays Casey alimony of $70,000 per year for a specified number of years. They have two children, who spend slightly more time with Casey, giving her head of household filing status. Dylan will file as single. For the sake of simplicity, we will leave any child support considerations out of this example. Also for the sake of simplicity, we will assume that both parties take only standard deductions.

Calculating Taxable Income for 2018:

If Dylan and Casey had finalized their settlement agreement in 2018, Dylan would have been able to take what is known as an “above-the-line” deduction for his alimony payments. $218,000 of income would be taxable ($300,000, minus $70,000 alimony, minus a $12,000 single filer standard deduction). He would be in the 35% tax bracket for single filers and pay $51,990 in federal tax ($45,689.50 plus 35% of the excess over $200,000). His after-tax income would therefore be **$178,010** ($300,000, minus taxes of $51,989, minus alimony of $70,000).

Casey, on the other hand, would have had to add the alimony payments to her 2018 income, giving her a new taxable income of $132,000 ($80,000, plus $70,000 in alimony, minus an $18,000 head of household deduction). This would put her in the 24% tax bracket for heads of household, and she would pay taxes of $24,578 ($12,698 plus 24% of the excess over $82,500). Her after tax income would therefore be **$125,422** ($150,000 minus taxes of $24,578).

Calculating Taxable Income for 2019 and Beyond:

If Casey and Dylan did not finalize their settlement agreement until 2019, with the same income and the same alimony payments, Dylan would have taxable income for 2019 of $287,800 ($300,000 minus $12,200 for the revised 2019 single filer deduction). He would remain in the 35% bracket and pay taxes of $75,924 ($46,628.50 plus 35% of the amount over $204,100). His new after-tax income on paper would be $224,076. After paying the $70,000 in alimony, however, he would only keep **$154,076.**

Casey's 2019 taxable income without adding the alimony payments would be only $61,650 ($80,000 minus $18,350 for the revised 2019 head of household deduction). This would drop her to the 22% bracket and she would pay taxes of only $8,001 ($6,065 plus 22% of the amount over $52,850), giving her an after-tax income on paper of $71,999. After receiving the $70,000 in alimony payments, however, she would actually have **$141,999.**

Effects on Total Income of Both Parties:

We do not need to go through the above analysis to show that one result of the Trump tax is that Dylan loses a tax break. The example highlights, however, how significant such breaks sometimes were for spouses with substantial earnings. With exactly the same earnings and the same alimony payment in 2019 as in 2018, Dylan's net income drops by **$23,934** ($154,076 compared to $178,010).

It initially appears that Casey has received a benefit, because the tax break has simply shifted to her. After all, in this example, the exact same earnings and alimony payments in 2019 as in 2018 have lifted her net income by **$16,577** ($141,999 compared to $125,422). For several reasons, however, it is unlikely that Casey would actually ever see this increase.

First of all, the calculation of an appropriate amount of alimony changes significantly given the change in after-tax effects. Dylan and other high income spouses who expect to pay alimony have an obvious new negotiating position. They will simply offer to pay less. If Dylan subtracts the amount of his lost tax break ($23,934) from what he would have otherwise agreed to pay ($70,000) and offers that lower amount instead ($46,066), he will end up in the same position as under the old rules.

Should Casey accept this lower offer, however, she will end up in a significantly worse position than under the old rules. This is because the less obvious, and in many ways more important, take-away that our example highlights is that the Trump tax can have a dramatic effect on the total combined after-tax income available to both former spouses. Notice that, in our example, Dylan's actual net income decreased in 2019 by $23,934, while Casey's actual net income increased by only $16,577, a difference of $7,357. Where did this $7,357 go? To the IRS.

Looking at this another way, under the 2018 analysis, Casey and Dylan's combined after-tax income is **$303,432**, while under the 2019 analysis, it is only **$296,075**. The couple as a whole therefore loses **$7,357** per year, or $613 per month. If Casey accepts Dylan's offer to pay an amount that compensates him for his lost tax break, this deficit will fall entirely on her. Spouses like Casey and the attorneys who represent them need to be aware of this hidden consequence of what initially appears to be a positive change for a spouse receiving alimony.

Married/Divorced Comparison:

Another way of looking at the effect of the new law is to compare the taxation of divorced couples to that of married couples:

If Dylan and Casey had remained married and filed taxes jointly in 2018, their combined gross income would be $380,000. After subtracting the 2018 standard deduction of $24,000 for joint filers, they would have taxable income of $356,000, on which they would pay taxes of $77,299 ($64,179 plus 32% of the excess over $315,000). They would therefore have a total combined after-tax income of $302,701, which is quite close to the combined after-tax total of $303,432 they would have if they filed separately with alimony payments.

If they filed jointly in 2019 on the same income, however, their taxable income would be $355,600 ($380,000 minus the 2019 standard deduction of $24,400) and they would pay taxes of $75,425 ($65,497 plus 32% of the amount over $321,450). Their total after-tax income would therefore be $303,575, which is significantly ($7,500) higher than the $296,075 of combined after-tax income the couple would have if they filed separately with alimony payments.

Comparing these different scenarios demonstrates that the real effect of shifting the tax burden of alimony payments to the party with a higher income is to penalize both divorced parties, whether they pay alimony or rely on it. This result seems especially unfair in light of the fact that divorced or single people generally need a tax break much more than married people do, since maintaining two households is considerably more expensive than maintaining one. The overall effect is something like a tax on divorce.

Because of the unpopularity of this recent change, there is a chance that it will at some point be reversed. Always seek the advice of both an attorney and a tax professional before finalizing any support agreement to be sure that you are aware of the current tax implications of all aspects of your agreement and that you are making the right decisions.

Chapter 2

Establishing Alimony in New Jersey

Each state has implemented different rules for categorizing and calculating alimony. While many states have similar rules, a particular set of circumstances might entitle a spouse to alimony in one state but not another, or might call for payment of a higher amount in one state than in another.

There are five different types of alimony that a court might order in New Jersey. These are: *pendente lite*, open durational, permanent, limited duration, rehabilitative, and reimbursement. Prior to the 2014 alimony reforms, open durational alimony was called permanent alimony, and was subject to somewhat different rules. Later in this chapter, we will look more closely at the differences between each type of alimony.

The Alimony Factors

When determining which type or types of alimony is appropriate in any particular case, a court must consider all of the circumstances, including but not limited to the following factors set out in the New Jersey alimony statute:

- The actual need and ability of the parties to pay;
- The duration of the marriage or civil union;
- The age, physical and emotional health of the parties;
- The standard of living established in the marriage or civil union and the likelihood that each party can maintain a reasonably comparable standard of living, with neither party having a greater entitlement to that standard of living than the other;
- The earning capacities, educational levels, vocational skills, and employability of the parties;
- The length of absence from the job market of the party seeking maintenance;
- The parental responsibilities for the children;

- The time and expense necessary to acquire sufficient education or training to enable the party seeking maintenance to find appropriate employment, the availability of the training and employment, and the opportunity for future acquisitions of capital assets and income;

- The history of the financial or non-financial contributions to the marriage or civil union by each party including contributions to the care and education of the children and interruption of personal careers or educational opportunities;

- The equitable distribution of property ordered and any payouts on equitable distribution, directly or indirectly, out of current income, to the extent this consideration is reasonable, just and fair;

- The income available to either party through investment of any assets held by that party;

- The tax treatment and consequences to both parties of any alimony award, including the designation of all or a portion of the payment as a non-taxable payment;

- The nature, amount, and length of *pendente lite* support paid, if any; and

  Any other factors which the court may deem relevant. N.J.S.A. 2A:34-23b.

The 2014 amendments to the statute make clear that any time a party requests alimony the court must consider all of the listed factors, and if any factor(s) are given more weight than others, must render a written opinion explaining the reasons for this.

Marital Fault Not Usually Considered

One factor New Jersey courts generally do not consider relevant to an alimony award is marital fault. Although there are still some states that take fault into account in determining whether or not a spouse is entitled to alimony, the trend across the country is toward discounting the importance of fault. Many states will not consider it at all. In New Jersey, the legal view is that once fault enters the picture, the likelihood of settlement is dramatically reduced.

There is a steep interest in encouraging settlement between the parties so that they can achieve a resolution without having to involve the courts, which institutions are already overly consumed with a backlog of cases to handle. By eliminating marital fault, the typical mud-slinging that comes along with it is removed from the equation so that the parties can look at the case more along the lines of a business decision that they have to make. When emotions related to adultery are intertwined with the need to divide assets for instance, a person having felt victimized by the infidelity may be unwilling to compromise. It is near impossible to simply cast aside one's feelings of betrayal, but when a party understands that a court will not take the infidelity factor into consideration, there is a greater chance of focusing the attention back toward necessary decision-making for settlement purposes.

There are a few limited situations, however, in which a New Jersey court might consider fault. One type of situation is where the behavior of one spouse was so egregious that an ordinary person would find it shocking to the conscience. While certain types of behavior clearly satisfy that standard (attempted murder of the spouse, for example), in less severe situations courts evaluate each case individually to determine whether behavior was sufficiently shocking to merit consideration. Although this standard is meant to be objective, and judges are supposed to base decisions on how they believe that a reasonable person would react to specific facts, in reality, it can be difficult to predict what kind of behavior any particular judge would consider to be so shocking that it crosses the line.

FAQs: Can we estimate alimony payments with a mathematical formula?

It is important to be aware that there is no legal formula for calculating alimony in New Jersey. Sometimes judges may apply "rules of thumb" formulas that are based on commonly accepted practices, but this is not something that is currently supported by the law. In fact, you will probably want to make sure that the judge in your case does not use a mathematical formula. Although judges who do this are making an effort to keep decisions more uniform, recent New Jersey case law indicates that reliance on such formulas may be legitimate grounds for appeal

Types of Alimony

Four of the five types of alimony New Jersey courts recognize come into play when a divorce is finalized. These are limited duration, open durational (formerly permanent), rehabilitative, and reimbursement alimony. The fifth type is alimony *pendente lite*, or temporary alimony, which a court may award during the course of a case, prior to a determination of whether or not any of the other four types would be appropriate.

Courts may award different types of alimony in combination. Although limited duration and open durational alimony are alternative forms of support and would not be appropriate in the same case, rehabilitative and reimbursement alimony have distinct purposes and a court can award both types together. Courts can also award either rehabilitative or reimbursement alimony (or both) in conjunction with limited duration or open durational alimony. The factors listed above are important in determining not only whether or not alimony is appropriate, but also what type of alimony is appropriate, what the amount should be, and for how long it should be paid.

If you are considering or in the process of a New Jersey divorce and are wondering whether or not you may have to pay alimony or may be entitled to receive alimony, you will need a thorough understanding of the different types of alimony and the different purpose each type is designed to serve. The following is a brief overview:

***Pendente Lite* Alimony:**

This is a form of temporary alimony with the main purpose of preserving the financial "status quo" of both spouses during the course of the case. In the alimony context "status quo" refers to the current financial state at the beginning of the divorce case. The most important factors in determining the amount of temporary alimony required to preserve the status quo will be one spouse's need and the other spouse's ability to pay, based on each spouse's current income and current expenses. Property distribution will not yet have occurred, and as such will not be a consideration. Tax treatment and concurrent payment of temporary child support will be important, however, as these may substantially affect the actual amount of money available to each spouse.

Several states use financial formulas to determine temporary alimony, often in conjunction with the calculation of temporary child support; however, New Jersey currently does not have such a formula. For this reason the calculation of temporary alimony, like all other types of alimony, can be unpredictable and can vary considerably from county to county and judge to judge.

Open Durational Alimony (formerly Permanent Alimony):

Orders and agreements predating September 10, 2014. If you have an alimony order or a marital settlement agreement dated prior to September 10, 2014, you may be paying or receiving permanent alimony. Permanent alimony is the most traditional form of alimony and was once quite common. It was eliminated in New Jersey and replaced with open durational alimony in the 2014 statutory amendments. Under New Jersey law prior to this change, permanent alimony generally came into play only after a long-term marriage. Its primary purpose was to help the spouse receiving it maintain a standard of living reasonably comparable to that which the couple enjoyed together during the marriage. Limiting permanent alimony to long-term marriages reflected the reality that in most cases, the longer a marriage, the greater each party's contribution, financial or otherwise, to the marital standard of living, and the more difficulty either party would have adjusting to living at a lower standard.

The pre-reform statute did not define exactly how long a marriage had to be to qualify as long-term. Some judges considered more than 10 years to be long-term, while others treated most marriages of 10 to 15 years as only intermediate in length. Other factors played a significant role in the determination, such as the ages of the parties. For instance, if a couple married in their early 20's and were married for 15 years (divorcing in their mid-30s), a permanent alimony award would have been less likely since it might have required support payments of potentially 30-plus years on a marriage only half that length of time. A key factor was the existence of a substantial disparity in income between the spouses throughout the marriage, resulting in one spouse developing a permanent economic dependency on the other. The amount of the award would always depend on the ability of the higher-earning spouse to pay the needed support.

Once a court determined that permanent alimony was appropriate because one spouse had been financially dependent on the other for many years, the focus shifted from how long alimony would last to how much a dependent spouse would require based on analysis of other relevant factors. The word "permanent," however, was always somewhat misleading. An order for permanent alimony did not prohibit the paying spouse from seeking a modification at a later date based on an assertion that circumstances had substantially changed and either the dependent spouse no longer needed the same amount or the paying spouse could no longer pay it.

Orders and agreements after September 10, 2014. The 2014 reforms to the alimony statute replaced permanent alimony with open durational alimony. As was the case with permanent alimony, the primary purpose of open durational alimony is to help the spouse receiving it maintain a standard of living reasonably comparable to that which the couple enjoyed together during the marriage. The primary difference is that under the revised statute, in the absence of exceptional circumstances, a court can award open-durational alimony only after a marriage of at least 20 years in length. The revision to the statute thus takes away the need for debate over the definition of a "long-term" marriage.

Like permanent alimony, open durational alimony has no set ending date. It will be easier to modify or terminate open durational alimony, however, because of other revisions to the statute, including a new presumption that all alimony awards end once the payer reaches full retirement age.

As with permanent alimony, the degree to which one spouse has become economically dependent on the other during the marriage will determine whether or not open durational alimony is appropriate and if so, what the amount ought to be. When one spouse has been a homemaker during the marriage and has no experience working outside the home, while the other spouse has built a lucrative career and can expect to continue earning a good income, the stay-at-home spouse's need for support will be clear. Judges, however, are also likely to find open durational support to be fair in a broad range of other scenarios in which permanent alimony sometimes came into play prior to the statutory revisions. For example, a spouse who had a successful career during the early years of a marriage, but acted as a homemaker or parent exclusively for the last several years may have to start a career over at the entry level, or may even find it difficult or impossible to re-enter the work force at all, consequently requiring at least some level of indefinite support. In some cases, the dependent spouse's advanced age or ill health may be an additional impediment to finding suitable employment and weigh in favor of keeping the term of the alimony award open.

Whether a dependent spouse has resumed a career after a long hiatus or has recently embarked on a new career, if it is unlikely that this career will ever result in a level of income that can support the spouse at a standard of living close to that of the marriage, an award of open duration may be appropriate. Where it is clear that the activities of one spouse in giving up career or educational opportunities to focus on homemaking or parenting facilitated the efforts of the other spouse in gaining advanced education or advanced career status, a court will also take this into account.

Courts can add reimbursement or rehabilitative alimony to open durational support in an appropriate case. A court will carefully consider how much time and expense is likely to be necessary for the dependent spouse to acquire additional education or training, to conduct a job search, and to advance to a suitable level in a new or resumed career. The extent to which the equitable distribution of property may compensate the dependent spouse will also be an important factor.

In these kinds of situations, the divorcing spouses will often disagree regarding the earning potential of the dependent spouse. This argument may be settled by obtaining the opinion of a qualified vocational evaluator. Each spouse can hire their own evaluator or they can agree to use a joint evaluator. Couples attempting to work out alimony arrangements on their own often hire a joint evaluator and agree to accept the evaluator's opinion as the basis for their agreement.

The new restriction limiting open durational awards to marriages of longer than 20 years is not absolute. A court could order open durational alimony in a shorter marriage in the presence of "exceptional circumstances." What exactly are exceptional circumstances? Rather than define them specifically, the statute leaves it to the courts to analyze the following second list of factors to determine whether or not such circumstances exist:

- The ages of the parties at the time of the marriage or civil union and at the time of the alimony award;

- The degree and duration of the dependency of one party on the other party during the marriage or civil union;

- Whether a spouse or partner has a chronic illness or unusual health circumstance;

- Whether a spouse or partner has given up a career or a career opportunity or otherwise supported the career of the other spouse or partner;

- Whether a spouse or partner has received a disproportionate share of the marital estate;

- The impact of the marriage or civil union on either party's ability to become self-supporting including but not limited to either party's responsibility as primary caretaker of a child;

- Tax considerations of either party;

- Any other factors or circumstances that the court deems equitable, relevant and material.
  N.J.S.A 2A:34-23c.

"When determining which type or types of alimony is appropriate in any particular case, a court must consider all of the circumstances."

Bari Z. Weinberger, Esq.

Limited Duration Alimony:

Limited duration alimony, also sometimes called "term alimony," is spousal support that a court orders for a predetermined length of time. In general, courts consider couples in short or intermediate length marriages to have made less of a joint commitment to the marital lifestyle and to have better opportunities to become self-sufficient following the marriage. In many cases, however, the same factors that would justify an open-ended alimony award after a longer marriage will also justify a limited duration award after a shorter-term marriage.

Under the revised law, only marriages of at least 20 years will qualify as long enough to justify an open-ended award, unless exceptional circumstances exist. Therefore, in most cases only limited duration alimony will be available following any marriage of less than 20 years. The term of limited duration alimony prior to the 2014 statutory revisions was primarily based on the length of the marriage and the income or income potential of each party, along with the other statutory factors. This is still the case, with one important caveat: Under the revised statute, in the absence of exceptional circumstances, limited duration support awards cannot exceed the length of the marriage. Courts will evaluate the existence of exceptional circumstances in this context by applying the same list of factors set out above (N.J.S.A. 2A:34-23c).

Rehabilitative Alimony:

Rehabilitative alimony is another type of support with a predetermined term, but in this case the specific purpose of the alimony is to fund a plan for the recipient to become self-sufficient or to at least productively enter the workforce. It can be awarded either separately or in conjunction with an award for reimbursement alimony and either open durational or term alimony. A dependent or lower earning spouse who does not have an established career or work history but has a plan to return to school or obtain some other type of training for a specific position or employment might qualify for this type of support. The award could include the tuition or cost of training, as well as costs of living during the training or education period and for a reasonable period of time afterward to allow the recipient time to obtain a job. A court will require a spouse requesting rehabilitation alimony to submit a detailed plan, including a time frame for completion of the plan and the specific amounts required along each step of the plan.

Reimbursement Alimony:

The final type of support is reimbursement alimony. This is a specific award of compensatory costs that one spouse may be entitled to as a result of supporting the other spouse during a period of graduate or professional education or training. The award can include not only tuition reimbursement, but also the costs of living expended by the student spouse during the period of education, as well as any other costs related to obtaining the degree or training.

An award of reimbursement alimony acknowledges that both spouses anticipated enjoying an increased standard of living from the advanced training or degree, and that the spouse who worked to fund the other spouse's education (sometimes forgoing additional personal education or career advancement potential to do so) will lose the anticipated benefit. Although reimbursement in this situation is classified as alimony, it is really a form of restitution. While some states recognize a property right in a degree or license that increases the earning potential of one spouse, New

Jersey does not. Reimbursement alimony is particularly appropriate in a short-term marriage where the couple has not yet raised their standard of living significantly or accumulated substantial property as a result of the increased earning potential. In a longer-term marriage, a court might address the inequity through the division of property or another form of alimony instead.

Reimbursement alimony alone sometimes seems inadequate to repair the inequity resulting from one spouse's sacrifice of the couple's increased long-term earning potential. The spouse may get the financial contribution back, but not the investment in time and emotional commitment. Courts can award reimbursement alimony in conjunction with open durational or limited duration alimony, but it can be difficult to justify the rationale for these other types of alimony in a shorter marriage. Couples ordinarily live a relatively modest lifestyle during the phase of earning the advanced training. The divorce may occur just prior to a big jump in standard of living. The problem most often arises in marriages that are not long enough to qualify for open durational alimony, and since both open durational and limited duration alimony are restricted to the standard of living during the marriage, the spouse who helped make the jump possible can be completely shut out from realizing any of the benefits of the higher standard.

Courts might have difficulty rationalizing an award of rehabilitative alimony in this type of situation also, as the spouse who paid for the higher education may already be "self-supporting." Nevertheless, judges have great discretion in how they weigh factors involved in awarding alimony, and where one spouse has supported the other's education and has also foregone personal career advancement or professional education, a court could consider ordering both reimbursement alimony and rehabilitative alimony to permit the spouse who paid for the partner's degree or supported their home during the period of education to obtain a similar type of advanced qualifications.

FAQs: Are you entitled to alimony?

This can be a complicated question with different possible answers depending on which factors a court considers more important. It is up to you to make your case by stressing factors that support your financial need. To help you consider how a court might analyze your needs, start by listing all of the following:

- Length of your marriage,
- Your health and age and any ways that these may impact your future ability to work,
- The difference between your income and your spouse's income,
- The value of your assets as opposed to your spouse's assets,
- Your earning ability,
- Any training or education you would need to improve your earning ability, the length of time it would take to get this, and about how much it would cost,
- Your contributions to the marriage that decreased your earning potential: whether or not you left a job or delayed entering the job market to keep house or stay home with children, and the length of time that you stayed home,

- The extent of the child care responsibilities you had prior to and expect to have after the divorce, and the potential impact on your ability to earn.

Practical Tip: Be thorough in assessing employability of a spouse who is not working or who could be working at a higher paying job.
Regardless of whether you will be paying alimony or receiving it, if your spouse is unemployed or underemployed, insist that the spouse's ability to work and potential income be taken into account when negotiating alimony. Use U.S. Department of Labor and Wage statistics as a source for fair imputation figures, and be sure to take into consideration a spouse's specialized training, skills, degrees, and education level. In some cases where employability is a real issue, you may need to hire a vocational or employment expert.

Establishing the Marital Standard of Living

A court generally establishes the marital standard of living through examination of each spouse's history of earnings and monthly expenses, as described in financial budgets the parties prepare for the case.

In New Jersey, the appropriate form for preparation of these budgets is the Case Information Statement (CIS). A complete description of the CIS appears in our companion e-book in this series, "Uncontested Divorce." How carefully you complete your CIS can have a substantial impact on the likelihood and potential amount of an alimony award in your case.

In Part D of the CIS, you will be required to provide detailed information about your monthly expenses based on the marital standard of living. This section should reflect, as closely as possible, the actual expenses of your married life. If you are requesting alimony, or if you are defending against a claim of alimony by your spouse, it is very important that you take great care in completing this part of your CIS. You can expect that you will have to explain your answers and produce documentary proof of the basis for the numbers if your case ends up in a trial or a hearing on spousal support. Accuracy is critical. While it is important to provide exact numbers whenever possible, if you must estimate, indicate that you have done so, and explain why you believe the estimate to be reliable. Be certain to categorize expenses as specifically as possible. For example, instead of providing one figure for "entertainment," try to break the number down into amounts for specific types of entertainment, such as "holiday gifts" or "vacation travel."

While accurate preparation of a CIS is essential in a court case, the CIS can also be one of the most important documents in mediation or negotiation between spouses who are trying to keep their divorce out of the courts. If you and your spouse are attempting to settle your case amicably, documenting all of the expenses of the marriage will make disagreements about actual expenditures much less likely and heighten the likelihood of resolution.

Documents that you may need to verify your monthly expenses include the following:

- checkbook registers or cancelled checks,
- credit card statements,
- utility bills,
- mortgage statements,
- personal loan documents (for automobiles, financed home furnishings, etc.).

An attorney can help you prepare your CIS, but you must be sure that you review all figures and documents personally, as you will be the one called upon to testify regarding accuracy if your matter ends up in court at any point. Make sure that you understand everything included in the CIS and that you would be able to explain the basis of each amount and provide documentary support.

Including All Expenses:

In describing expenses, it is important to include items that many people would not consider to be "necessary." For example, if during your marriage you and your spouse saved a considerable amount each year, or travelled to expensive locales, or threw extravagant parties on a regular basis, these activities were elements of your overall marital lifestyle and therefore constitute an element of need for purposes of analyzing the marital standard of living.

Addressing Variations in the Standard of Living over Time:

Expenses are rarely completely stable from year to year. Where a couple's standard of living has increased over time, a spouse who is anticipating having to pay alimony may want to average expenses and income back for a considerable period to make it appear that the overall standard of living during the marriage has been lower than the current standard. While it is usually necessary to average over some length of time to get an accurate picture, if the standard of living has been increasing and would be expected to continue increasing on a similar trajectory, a spouse seeking alimony should argue that any lowering that occurs by averaging back is illusory. It would be particularly inappropriate to consider years during which the high-earning spouse was attending school or working in an entry level position, or the lean start up years of a business that is currently thriving.

On the other hand, if a business has suffered a recent loss, or the high earning spouse has made a recent job change and is now earning less, the stability of the standard of living may be difficult to gauge. The lower income could be due to temporary uncontrollable factors, or to uncontrollable factors that are likely to persist for a significant period of time. It could also be due to controllable factors representing lifestyle choices by one or both spouses. Similarly, if income has increased sharply in just the past two or three years of a long marriage, the high earning spouse could argue that these recent years do not represent the true marital standard. There is no black and white rule establishing how long a couple has to live at a particular standard of living before that standard should form the basis for an alimony claim. An experienced family law attorney can help you prepare an argument supporting your case whether you are the spouse needing support or the spouse who is expecting to pay it.

"A court generally establishes the marital standard of living through examination of each spouse's history of earnings and monthly expenses."

Bari Z. Weinberger, Esq.

Practical Tip: Need is a critical factor.
Remember that a court will not order one spouse to pay alimony, regardless of the spouse's wealth or extremely high earning power, unless the other spouse actually needs the alimony to avoid a significant drop in standard of living.

Litigating the Marital Standard of Living

For couples that are having difficulty agreeing on an appropriate amount of alimony, the marital standard of living may be a sticking point. If your spouse has a very different perception of what the standard of living has been during the marriage, it can be difficult to decide whether it makes more sense to continue trying to compromise or to proceed to litigation. The costs of litigating this issue can be very high, and where there are arguments supporting different points of view, a judge's decision may seem rather arbitrary.

While attorney assistance will be important in deciding what kind of settlement is reasonable in such a case, there are a few basic things to keep in mind:

Total Resources Available

In the great majority of divorces, a couple lacks sufficient income to enable both spouses to maintain the same lifestyle formerly enjoyed in one household after separating into two, and the emphasis will instead be on ensuring that the drop in standard of living does not fall disparately on only one party. The availability of alimony as a remedy depends not only on need, but also on ability to pay, and fairness demands that any shortfall be shared. If you believe there will be adequate cash flow to allow both spouses to maintain the marital standard of living following divorce, it is important to demonstrate this carefully. If it is apparent that there will not be an adequate cash flow, you must accept that each of you will have to make some concessions.

Overall Life Circumstances

Courts tend to take a fairly broad viewpoint in looking at standards of living. While a precise accounting of income and expenses is necessary to support a standard of living argument, a court is likely to make decisions based primarily on overall circumstances, such as whether a couple generally lived an upper, middle, or upper-middle class lifestyle. A spouse requesting alimony should consider how much money is necessary to maintain the same general kind of lifestyle without major adjustment, rather than just thinking about the maximum amount of income available.

Knowledge about Recent Local Court Decisions

Because alimony awards can be based on so many different factors, different judges may order widely varying amounts. Trends sometimes develop in local areas that are not necessarily reliable in predicting outcomes outside those areas. A family law attorney with extensive experience representing parties at a local family courthouse will often be familiar with the tendencies and histories of the different judges and will consequently be able to give you a better estimate regarding a potential decision once your case has been assigned to a judge. Negotiating an amount without this kind of attorney assistance may save you legal fees, but it also may leave you without the "insider knowledge" that can be so valuable to assessing the right settlement value in your case, creating a long-term financial impact.

Expert Opinions

In some cases, expert testimony may be necessary to support an argument regarding the marital standard of living. A forensic accountant can present an analysis of all factors over a period of years to create a picture of the lifestyle from year to year. You and your spouse can each hire separate experts, or you can use a joint expert. Using a joint expert can result in significant savings, and may also help you reach a settlement. An attorney can help you decide whether or not the use of a forensic accountant would be cost effective in your case, and if so, whether retaining a joint expert is a reasonable option.

Litigation Costs

The costs of litigation are extremely high. If you have financial need and are seeking alimony, you may be able to get your spouse to cover some of your litigation costs. However, keep in mind that not everyone who believes that they should be entitled to attorney's fees will get them, and, regardless of which one of you pays the attorneys, the money must come out of the total amount available to both of you for all purposes, including property division, alimony, and if applicable, child support. This is a particularly critical concern when it is apparent that the available income will necessitate a drop in standard of living. Unfortunately, litigating this type of case sometimes simply increases the size of the drop for one or both parties. Where both spouses are capable of reasonable negotiation, an amicable settlement can maximize results for everyone.

Practical Tip: Watch out for discretionary payments, such as discretionary trust income, when calculating support.

Courts include most sources of income as potentially available for alimony payments. Always check with a knowledgeable attorney, however, before assuming that you will or will not be able to count any unusual sources. Courts generally will not include income if access to the income is not under the control of the spouse who will be responsible for paying support. For example, some people receive payments from discretionary trusts. Because this income is neither guaranteed nor related to the efforts of the person receiving it, a court may not include it when calculating a basic alimony obligation. When something like bonus income is fairly well established but not guaranteed, a court may order payment of a percentage of any future amounts. There are many complex scenarios involving income and alimony where the advice of an attorney is critical to an accurate analysis. In many cases, you will need the services of a financial professional to help you evaluate these scenarios as well.

Chapter 3

Agreements Affecting Alimony

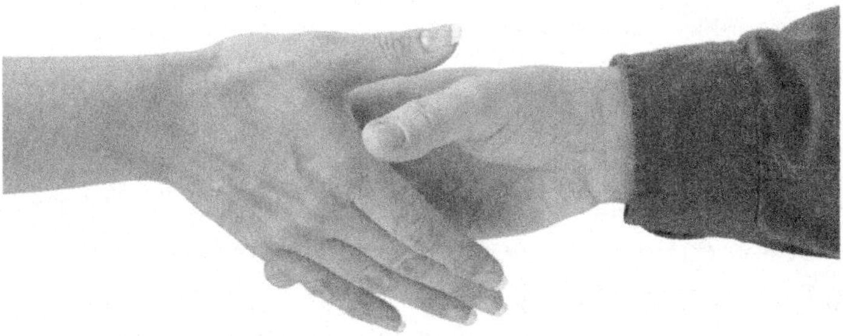

There are three different types of agreements between couples that may impact the payment of alimony after divorce.

- *Prenuptial (or premarital) agreements,*
- *Postnuptial (or mid-marriage) agreements, and*
- *Marital settlement agreements.*

Alimony and Prenuptial or Postnuptial Agreements

Prenuptial or premarital agreements are legal contracts that some couples enter into before marriage to define what will happen with their assets and income in the event of a divorce. Postnuptial or midmarriage agreements are similar, except that they are entered into during marriage. Both types of agreement can define the terms under which one spouse will (or will not) pay alimony to the other. There are very specific requirements, however, that must be followed in order to ensure that agreements will be enforceable in court. These requirements are slightly different for prenuptial agreements than for postnuptial agreements.

If you are considering putting terms about alimony into either a prenuptial or postnuptial agreement, it is imperative that you consult with an attorney. If you have either type of an agreement and are now in the process of obtaining a divorce, you should have an attorney review the terms of the agreement to assess its enforceability.

An open question following recent changes in tax law is whether or not such changes will affect alimony terms in existing prenuptial or postnuptial agreements. Since alimony was deductible by the payer for many decades, any couple with an existing agreement for payment of a specific amount of alimony in the event of a hypothetical divorce was in all likelihood assuming such deductibility when negotiating the terms, regardless of whether or not their agreement states this explicitly. Unless they now revise or clarify the terms with a postnuptial agreement, they risk an unintended result in the event of a divorce.

If you are happily married, it may seem unnecessarily disruptive to revisit the topic of potential divorce. Nevertheless, if the fact that alimony was to be tax deductible is important to you and did influence your agreement to pay (how much or for how long), then you may want to consider asking your spouse to sign a postnup renegotiating the terms. A postnup could address the change in tax law and allow you and your spouse, for example, to equalize the difference between what you expected to pay, and what will be paid if you divorce after 2018.

If you have a prenuptial or postnuptial agreement that predates 2019 and contains alimony terms, contact a family law attorney for assistance in deciding whether or not you may need to revise your agreement. You can find more information regarding such agreements and the potential impact they may have on alimony payments, in our companion book in this series, entitled "*A Guide To Relationship Agreements In New Jersey.*"

Alimony and Marital Settlement Agreements

Divorcing couples generally use marital settlement agreements (also sometimes called "property settlement agreements") to detail the division of their assets and debts. In appropriate cases, such agreements can include a schedule for payment of alimony, as well as a list of specific conditions that would lead to termination or reduction of alimony. Every divorcing couple who agrees to terms including payment of alimony without going to court needs to finalize a written marital settlement agreement and file the agreement in court. Any party who has not done this will have difficulty enforcing payment of alimony.

Whether or not a court will enforce alimony terms in a marital settlement agreement depends on the exact language used in the agreement, whether the agreement as a whole has been properly executed, and whether the terms themselves are fair. While courts generally strive to uphold terms couples have agreed to voluntarily, they will not uphold terms that unduly restrict either spouse. For example, a court might enforce an agreement stating that alimony will end if the recipient cohabits with another adult in a relationship tantamount to marriage for a certain amount of time regardless of the lack of economic impact from the cohabitation, but a court would not uphold an agreement that prohibits a recipient from dating.

The conditions under which courts may or may not uphold terms in marital settlement agreements can be difficult to predict. In recent years, courts have gone back and forth in their interpretations of laws governing how various types of agreements between couples can affect the ability of a court to award alimony and decide on the appropriate amount. Since the exact language of an agreement expressing contingencies in alimony payments is so important, a couple who wishes to include such terms in a marital settlement agreement should always consult with an attorney.

Parties will also frequently insert a clause in a marital settlement agreement preventing modification of agreed terms regarding alimony even if circumstances change in the future. These are sometimes called "*Anti-Lepis*" clauses, based on the name of a leading New Jersey alimony modification case. While courts often uphold *Anti-Lepis* clauses, this type of clause must also be written in very clear and specific language. Attorney advice is a must to ensure an effective clause.

Questions about "Palimony" Agreements

If you are not married but you are ending a relationship with someone you have been living with, you may wonder if you are entitled to alimony or if you will have to pay alimony. The answer is no; alimony laws in New Jersey only apply to married couples. Over the years, there have been many court decisions, both in New Jersey and in other states, addressing the issue of whether or not there can be any obligation of support running between partners who are not married, but who have been in a marriage-like relationship. These are sometimes called "palimony" claims.

Palimony claims have generally been seen in relationships where one partner has become financially dependent on the other. The dependent partner claims that the supporting partner made a promise to continue providing financial support even after the end of the relationship. While the law regarding palimony in New Jersey has gone through several changes over time, an amendment to the New Jersey Statute of Frauds that went into effect on January 18, 2010 now provides that courts can enforce this type of promise between unmarried partners only if the parties put their agreement into writing (N.J.S.A. 25:1-5 (2013)). In 2014, the New Jersey Supreme Court, in the case of *Maeker v. Ross* (99 A. 3d 795, 219 NJ 565), clarified that parties with an oral agreement predating the amendment can still attempt to prove their terms in court.

Palimony agreements are also sometimes referred to as "cohabitation agreements." Following the amendment to the Statute of Frauds, in order to be valid, a cohabitation agreement must be signed by both partners and each of them must have received advice from separate attorneys at the time they entered into the agreement. You can learn more about Cohabitation Agreements in our companion e-book in this series, "*A Guide To Relationship Agreements In New Jersey.*"

Whether or not you have this type of written agreement, if you believe that your former live-in partner owes you a share of money or property, you should consult with an experienced attorney to find out if you have any basis for a claim. Even without an agreement you may have a claim based on property law. There are also several equitable grounds (based in principles of basic fairness) that could potentially apply in your case. The law in New Jersey with respect to palimony remains somewhat unsettled. In general, however, if you are not married and you do not have a written agreement, you will not have a claim for support.

Practical Tip: Consider all potential tax consequences of alimony payments when negotiating agreements.

Always consult with an accountant or CPA before finalizing any agreements affecting payment of alimony. There are many possible pitfalls. Recent changes in the federal tax code mean that alimony ordered or agreed upon in 2019 or later will be treated differently than alimony ordered or agreed upon in earlier years. This is a change that has not yet been tested and could therefore have unanticipated ramifications. A financial professional will be up to date on any recent IRS decisions that could affect the potential tax consequences of your agreement.

"There are three different types of agreements between couples that may impact the payment of alimony after divorce: prenuptial, postnuptial and marital settlement agreements."

Bari Z. Weinberger, Esq.

Chapter 4

Special Alimony Considerations for Military Spouses

Military spouses must often confront unique issues when facing divorce. These may involve complicated questions about which state laws apply when the parties have moved around frequently due to changes in duty location or deployment. They may also concern the interplay between state and federal laws.

Though state laws govern divorces, certain federal laws can affect aspects of divorce for military personnel. For example, The Uniformed Services Former Spouses' Protection Act (USFSPA) allows state courts to divide military pensions in divorce, but the applicable state law will determine exactly *how* military pay and pensions are split between the former spouses.

If you are serving or have served in the military, or you are married to someone who is serving or has served in the military, it is imperative that you have an attorney who is familiar with military divorce. The following points will provide you some idea of where to start when confronting the issue of alimony in a military divorce:

Branch Regulations

The Air Force, Army, Marine Corps, and Navy all have slightly different regulations governing payment of child and spousal support in the absence of a court order or legal agreement between spouses. For example, the Navy uses equations requiring payment of different percentages of gross pay depending on whether there is a spouse only (one-third), a child only (one-sixth), a spouse and one child (one-half), and so on. The Army employs equations that vary depending on living arrangements and military or non-military status of the spouse, while the Air Force does not use equations at all and simply requires payment of adequate support, deferring to state courts for calculation. If you are seeking information about a particular branch of service, always be sure you have the most up-to-date versions of applicable regulations.

It is generally best to rely on branch regulations only for temporary support. If you do not have an agreement or court order, and you are having difficulty obtaining support from a military spouse, you may be able to obtain assistance through the military command structure for the appropriate branch; however, obtaining relief in state court will generally provide you with superior protection as well as the ability to garnish wages for support. An attorney who practices military family law can provide additional information and will also be able to estimate the amount of support you might receive.

Calculating Available Income

Calculating income available for support from a servicemember's pay can be complicated. In New Jersey, benefits provided to the servicemember without cost in lieu of pay, such as a food or housing allowance, are included in the servicemember's gross income available for support. Accurate calculation of gross income requires imputing an appropriate amount for any such items, as well as examining the servicemember's LES to be sure that both basic pay and any special pay such as jump pay, dive pay, or flight pay is included.

Enforcing Military Support Payments

Due to the urgency involved in ensuring temporary support for children and dependent spouses, in some cases it may be possible to obtain a court order for temporary support even if the servicemember is attempting to stay the divorce proceedings under the Servicemembers Civil Relief Act. The servicemember may be able to participate in a temporary support hearing by telephone conference. A competent attorney can provide assistance.

If necessary, wage garnishment can be effected through the Department of Finance and Accounting Service (DFAS). You will need an order from the court directing the government to pay the spousal support amount and deduct it from the servicemember's earnings. Fortunately, default on a support obligation by a military servicemember is a relatively uncommon occurrence, perhaps due to military guidelines which could justify a dishonorable discharge due to the default, or perhaps simply because of the high standards of honor and integrity generally attributable to individuals in the service.

Military families can find more information at the American Bar Association's "HomeFront" website located at http://bit.ly/abahomefront.

Chapter 5

Enforcing Payment of Alimony

For alimony payments to be enforceable in court, the recipient must have either a court order directing payment or a properly executed marital settlement agreement. Settlement agreements must be signed by both parties; one party (either spouse) then files the agreement in court. The judge will usually attach the agreement to the judgment of divorce.

Setting Up Payments

While many former spouses honor their agreements fully and freely, there are some who will not. Sometimes life circumstances intervene and make it difficult or impossible to comply with financial obligations. In that case, a payer may be able to seek modification or termination of the obligation in court. This will be discussed in the next chapter. In other cases, a payer may feel that an alimony award was unfair and may simply avoid making payments out of resentment.

To avoid potential problems arising from failure to comply with alimony orders, an alimony recipient can request payment of alimony by wage garnishment and direct deposit (the payment is deposited directly into the recipient's bank account). Many couples who enter into settlement agreements find it less confrontational to agree instead on payment by personal check. Only the alimony recipient can judge whether or not this creates too big a risk of nonpayment.

Wage garnishment is handled by the county probation department. Employers are required to deduct support payments directly from an employee's paycheck and send them to the New Jersey Family Support Payment Center for release to the legal recipient. If you are a New Jersey alimony recipient who is not receiving payments on time from the payer, and you do not already have this type of arrangement, you can contact the probation department at your county courthouse for more information.

If you are the party responsible for paying alimony, you must understand that this is a serious legal obligation. If you are having difficulty keeping up payments due to job loss or another personal hardship, you should consult an attorney about making a request for a modification. Failing to do this could result in any or all of the consequences outlined below.

If you need help in reorganizing your finances so that you can pay your support obligations and your other debits, you should consult with a credit counselor, a financial advisor, or an attorney to help you find options. Filing for bankruptcy may help you with other debts but it will not ameliorate your responsibility for paying support. An alimony obligation takes priority over many other types of debt and is not dischargeable in bankruptcy. You will need to file a request for modification or termination of alimony in court if a change in your financial circumstances has rendered you unable to pay alimony under a current order or agreement.

Filing a Motion in Court

If you have stopped receiving alimony payments on time, you may have to file a "Motion to Enforce Litigants' Rights" in court. The superior court has the authority to order the party responsible for paying alimony to bring all payments up to date, make future payments on time, and pay any attorney's fees the recipient has incurred in bringing the motion.

The courts also have various tools available for ensuring compliance with orders for enforcement. A judge may be able to add part of an arrearage (past due support amount) to a regular wage-garnishment. If the non-paying party is unemployed but has substantial assets, the support recipient can ask the court to record the past due support amount as a judgment and direct the sheriff to seize assets such as bank accounts, or liquidate and sell other assets to satisfy the judgment. A recorded money judgment will also operate as a lien on any real estate the party owns.

In the most serious cases where a payer repeatedly disregards orders to bring payments up to date, a judge can issue a bench warrant for the party's arrest. This is a drastic remedy. Being in jail does not improve a party's ability to pay and may in fact considerably increase the difficulty. Nevertheless, the threat of jail time does sometimes succeed in conveying the seriousness of the situation to a defaulting party when other methods have failed.

Chapter 6

Modification or Termination of Alimony

For many fortunate people, entry of a final divorce decree means that everything connected with the former marriage has been settled once and for all. For others, the divorce decree brings closure and the ability to move on, but does not remove the possibility that loose ends may need additional attention in the future.

A divorce case is unlike most other lawsuits in that even after the parties have resolved all issues and the judge has entered a final judgment, matters commonly arise that require the former spouses to engage in additional settlement negotiations or even appear in court.

The court entering a final judgment of divorce will maintain jurisdiction over payment of alimony until a designated termination date, or indefinitely in the case of permanent or open durational alimony. This means that the court retains the power to make changes to alimony orders whenever there is a substantial change in circumstances after entry of the initial orders. In general, courts will not modify orders post-judgment unless the change in circumstances has already occurred and is expected to continue indefinitely or for at least a considerable length of time.

As a general rule, once a divorce is final and a couple has entered into a marital settlement agreement or a judge has ordered alimony payments, the amount and terms of payment are modifiable only if one spouse can show that circumstances have changed substantially and that the change is likely to be permanent. Other factors may also affect modifiability, including the type of alimony, the terms of the initial order, and the existence of any agreements between the parties regarding modification. Within the scope of these potential restrictions, a former spouse who is paying alimony can file a motion requesting a decrease, suspension, or termination of the obligation, or a recipient can file a motion requesting an increase, or a reinstatement of a suspended payment.

The death of either spouse will terminate an alimony obligation. Most types of alimony will also end if the recipient remarries or enters into a new civil union. Under some circumstances, specifically defined in the new amendments to the alimony statute, a recipient's cohabitation with a new partner can be the basis for reduction or modification. The new amendments also create a presumption that alimony will terminate once the paying spouse reaches full retirement age under the Social Security Act. Other situations may or may not be a legitimate ground for a modification, depending on all of the circumstances.

Modification or Termination of Alimony by Type

Pendente Lite Alimony

Pendente lite alimony is temporary by its very nature. It will terminate once the divorce is final and a settlement agreement or a new order granting or denying alimony takes effect. While the case is pending, however, either party can generally seek a modification based on the same kinds of changes in circumstances that might call for modification of a permanent, open durational, or limited duration alimony award.

Permanent Alimony (orders and agreements predating September 10, 2014)

As previously noted, the word "permanent" in the context of alimony payments has always been misleading. It refers to the lack of a predetermined termination date for payments, rather than to perpetual and unalterable payments. Both the duration and the amount of a permanent alimony award are modifiable on a showing that changed circumstances have either substantially impaired the paying spouse's ability to continue payments or resulted in a decreased need for support by the receiving spouse.

Open Durational Alimony (orders and agreements after September 10, 2014)

Like orders for permanent alimony, orders for open durational alimony have no predetermined ending date. As further discussed below, open durational alimony will be easier to modify or terminate than permanent alimony was, due to other changes in the revised statute relating to circumstances such as the paying spouse's retirement or loss of income, or the recipient spouse's cohabitation with a new partner.

Limited Duration Alimony

Limited duration alimony awards include a predetermined termination date. A judge can modify the amount of a limited duration award if there is a substantial change in circumstances, and can even extend the term of the award. In most respects, limited duration awards are subject to modification or termination on the same bases as permanent or open durational awards. Limited duration awards are sometimes based in whole or in part on events that the parties assume will occur at a particular time in the future. For instance, alimony may be awarded in a particular case until the youngest child graduates from high school.

Rehabilitative Alimony

A rehabilitative alimony award is also generally based on events the parties anticipate happening at predetermined times in the future. If circumstances change and the anticipated events fail to occur, a court may find modification appropriate. For example, if a spouse is receiving funds for tuition and living expenses necessary to complete an educational program designed to lead to improved employment prospects, and the spouse drops out of the program without completing it, the paying spouse can request relief from the payment obligation.

A spouse who expected to be fully employed within several months, or expected to reach a certain pay level within a couple of years, and was receiving rehabilitative alimony to bridge that gap may file a motion requesting additional alimony if economic factors beyond the spouse's control have interfered with the anticipated achievements. If it appears likely that the lack of full employment will last for a significant period of time, a judge can turn an award or agreement for rehabilitative alimony into an award for limited duration or possibly even open durational alimony.

Reimbursement Alimony

Because reimbursement alimony is a form of repayment, it is not subject to modification for any reason. As of September 10, 2014, this is explicitly stated in the revised statute.

Practical Tip: Do not put off addressing a change of circumstances situation.

While a court will not address a change of circumstances claim until after the circumstances have actually occurred, once the new circumstances are in place, it is important to bring a claim promptly (with a few potential exceptions). People who wait months or even years before seeking a modification of support will generally find themselves shut out from the possibility of receiving retroactive relief.

Proof Required

When alimony payments are modifiable by type and there are no restrictive agreements or orders, the court will take all relevant factors into account. Some of the scenarios that might call for modification under certain circumstances include the following:

- an increase in costs of living for the supported spouse,
- an increase in either spouse's income,
- a decrease in either spouse's income due to uncontrollable factors, such as a job lay-off, a new illness or disability, or the failure of a business despite diligent efforts,
- loss of living quarters due to foreclosure or eviction,
- cohabitation by the supported spouse, and
- either spouse's retirement from the work-force.

In most situations, the initial burden of producing evidence that a change of circumstances has occurred is on the party seeking a modification. The opposite will be true, however, when a paying spouse with an award or agreement post-dating September 10, 2014 reaches full retirement age; the burden will then fall on the recipient spouse to prove that the alimony should continue. Judges considering requests for modification or termination of alimony will look at sources of income for both parties, including not only actual income, but also any benefits that may reduce living costs, as well as assets that might be available to create a stream of income.

Evidence normally includes updated Case Information Statements (CIS), recent tax returns, and W-2 statements or business records.

The following is more information regarding evidence required to prove the need for a modification, suspension or termination of alimony in specific situations:

Requesting a Decrease in Payments

For a judge to consider a motion for a decrease or termination of alimony payments, the payer must generally demonstrate either a "good faith" decrease in ability to pay or a decrease in the recipient's need for the current amount of support. A good faith decrease in ability to pay is generally any decrease that was not voluntary and was not intentionally engineered for the purpose of avoiding the support obligation. For example, a court would not ordinarily permit a paying spouse who wishes to change to a lower paying career out of personal preference alone to reduce alimony payments.

Job Loss

If the decrease is due to job loss or a pay-cut, the applicant will also need to provide documentation supporting efforts to become re-employed at the former level, or evidence supporting a claim that such re-employment is not possible. Proof that an applicant is doing everything possible to become fully employed would include an updated resume, and a log demonstrating actual efforts to find work. The log should have dates, times, contact names and methods of contact (phone, email, interview, attendance at networking event, etc.). Conducting a very aggressive job search and keeping detailed records of results is a must. Statistical evidence demonstrating lack of appropriate work is also important. An attorney can provide you with advice on how best to present such a claim and what the best timing is likely to be.

Because the courts generally require a showing that available income has decreased permanently, or at least indefinitely, judges have often denied requests for decreases in payments filed after brief periods of unemployment on the grounds that such changes in circumstances may be only temporary. In a weak economic climate, on the other hand, some courts have been more likely to accept that a job loss will be long-term even when it has occurred relatively recently. The new amendments to the alimony statute attempt to resolve these discrepancies by providing that 90 days is the minimum period of unemployment required before a party can file an application for modification of alimony on that basis. The amendments further direct courts evaluating the income loss of a non-self-employed person to consider the following specific factors relating to all changes in financial circumstances of both parties since the award:

- The reasons for any loss of income;

- Under circumstances where there has been a loss of employment, the obligor's documented efforts to obtain replacement employment or to pursue an alternative occupation;

- Under circumstances where there has been a loss of employment, whether the obligor is making a good faith effort to find remunerative employment at any level and in any field;

- The income of the obligee; the obligee's circumstances; and the obligee's reasonable efforts to obtain employment in view of those circumstances and existing opportunities;

- The impact of the parties' health on their ability to obtain employment;

- Any severance compensation or award made in connection with any loss of employment;

- Any changes in the respective financial circumstances of the parties that have occurred since the date of the order from which modification is sought;

- The reasons for any change in either party's financial circumstances since the date of the order from which modification is sought, including, but not limited to, assessment of the extent to which either party's financial circumstances at the time of the application are attributable to enhanced earnings or financial benefits received from any source since the date of the order;

- Whether a temporary remedy should be fashioned to provide adjustment of the support award from which modification is sought, and the terms of any such adjustment, pending continuing employment investigations by the unemployed spouse or partner; and

- Any other factor the court deems relevant to fairly and equitably decide the application.
  N.J.S.A. 2A:34-23k

Under the amendments, a court has discretion to award either a permanent termination or reduction, or a temporary suspension or reduction pending ongoing efforts of the obligor to regain income. As always, non-self-employed obligors are expected to document good-faith efforts to become re-employed. Self-employed obligors must provide a business analysis comparing current economic and non-economic benefits to benefits that existed at the time of the entry of the alimony order. The court has the power to make the modification retroactive to the initial date of the loss of income.

Retirement

One of the most impactful changes implemented by the 2014 amendments concerns the way that courts will now address an obligor's retirement from the workforce. The amendments create a rebuttable presumption in favor of terminating alimony payments once an obligor has reached full retirement age under the Social Security Act. This is a change from previous law requiring an obligor to prove that retirement constituted a substantial change in circumstances. A recipient can overcome the new presumption in favor of termination by proving that alimony should continue based on the following specific factors:

- The ages of the parties at the time of the application for retirement;

- The ages of the parties at the time of the marriage or civil union and their ages at the time of entry of the alimony award;

- The degree and duration of the economic dependency of the recipient upon the payor during the marriage or civil union;

- Whether the recipient has foregone or relinquished or otherwise sacrificed claims, rights or property in exchange for a more substantial or longer alimony award;

- The duration or amount of alimony already paid;

- The health of the parties at the time of the retirement application;

- Assets of the parties at the time of the retirement application;

- Whether the recipient has reached full retirement age as defined in this section;

- Sources of income, both earned and unearned, of the parties;

- The ability of the recipient to have saved adequately for retirement; and

- Any other factors that the court may deem relevant. N.J.S.A. 2A:23-34j (1)

The amendments further state that courts should not consider the original asset distribution from the divorce when determining an obligor's ability to pay alimony following retirement. This relates to all types of retirement applications, both predating and post-dating the amendments. It prevents double-counting of certain assets. For example, if one spouse receives a share of the other's pension as part of a distribution of property in divorce, any income that is subsequently generated from the share retained by the paying spouse cannot be considered when calculating that spouse's ability to pay alimony after retirement. *(Stansbury v. Stansbury, NJ: Appellate Div. 2018).*

A judge who decides that a recipient has succeeded in overcoming the presumption in favor of termination must put the supporting findings of fact and conclusions of law into writing, and then apply all of the factors involved in the original determination of alimony (listed in N.J.S.A. 2A:34-23b) to the parties' present circumstances before making a final decision regarding whether termination or modification is appropriate. The amendments also allow courts to establish conditions for future retirement if the obligor intends to retire but has not yet done so. Prior to the amendments, a paying spouse contemplating retirement generally had to wait to file a motion for modification until after the actual retirement, as otherwise the change in circumstances would not yet have occurred and the possible effects were considered speculative. This made planning extremely difficult. Although the court process will now be considerably streamlined, when a paying spouse is facing retirement, it will still behoove both parties to attempt to reach an agreement regarding the impact of the retirement and avoid the stress and expense of going to court.

Retirement, particularly when it is several years or even decades in the future, can be difficult to plan for in advance, but negotiating an approach to this event during divorce settlement discussions can be helpful in avoiding future confrontation and legal fees. If at all possible, couples should strive to include contingencies for retirement in their marital settlement agreements.

“To decrease or terminate alimony, the payer must demonstrate either a ‘good faith’ decrease in ability to pay or a decrease in the need for the current amount of support.”

Bari Z. Weinberger, Esq.

Retirement with an Order or Agreement Predating the Effective Date of the 2014 Amendments

Prior to the 2014 amendments, New Jersey case law had established that a good faith retirement at the full retirement age of approximately 65 might call for a modification or reduction of permanent or limited duration alimony, but did not trigger any automatic termination or reduction. If the paying spouse had attained a reasonable retirement age for his or her industry and presented good faith reasons for the retirement, the court would hold a hearing to determine whether a reduction in support was appropriate.

The new presumption favoring termination applies only to prospective awards and retirement of an obligor at the statutorily defined full retirement age. An obligor who seeks to retire at full retirement age, but has an award that predates the amendments, is entitled only to a new statutory presumption that the retirement is in good faith. The court will then look at whether or not the recipient has had an opportunity to save for retirement, and will also consider yet another newly specified list of factors to determine whether the obligor has demonstrated that modification or termination is appropriate. These factors are:

- The age and health of the parties at the time of the application;

- The obligor's field of employment and the generally accepted age of retirement for those in that field;

- The age when the obligor becomes eligible for retirement at the obligor's place of employment, including mandatory retirement dates or the dates upon which continued employment would no longer increase retirement benefits;

- The obligor's motives in retiring, including any pressures to retire applied by the obligor's employer or incentive plans offered by the obligor's employer;

- The reasonable expectations of the parties regarding retirement during the marriage or civil union and at the time of the divorce or dissolution;

- The ability of the obligor to maintain support payments following retirement, including whether the obligor will continue to be employed part-time or work reduced hours;

- The obligee's level of financial independence and the financial impact of the obligor's retirement upon the obligee; and

- Any other relevant factors affecting the parties' respective financial position.
  N.J.S.A. 2A:34-23j (3)

Retirement before Full Retirement Age

In some states, if the paying spouse retires voluntarily before the age of 65, a court will not consider a request for alimony reduction based on the retirement. In other states, including New Jersey, early retirement is not an absolute bar to the reduction, but a court will examine the reasons for the retirement much more closely. An obligor who seeks to retire before full retirement age retains the full burden of demonstrating by a preponderance of the evidence that the retirement is reasonable and in good faith. Under the new statutory amendments, courts analyzing this type of situation will also look at whether or not the recipient has had an opportunity to save for retirement, and examine a separate list of factors set out in the amendments, as follows:

- The age and health of the parties at the time of the application;

- The obligor's field of employment and the generally accepted age of retirement for those in that field;

- The age when the obligor becomes eligible for retirement at the obligor's place of employment, including mandatory retirement dates or the dates upon which continued employment would no longer increase retirement benefits;

- The obligor's motives in retiring, including any pressures to retire applied by the obligor's employer or incentive plans offered by the obligor's employer;

- The reasonable expectations of the parties regarding retirement during the marriage or civil union and at the time of the divorce or dissolution;

- The ability of the obligor to maintain support payments following retirement, including whether the obligor will continue to be employed part-time or work reduced hours;

- The obligee's level of financial independence and the financial impact of the obligor's retirement upon the obligee; and

  Any other relevant factors affecting the obligor's decision to retire and the parties' respective financial positions.
  N.J.S.A. 2A:34-23j (2).

Remarriage

The remarriage of a spouse paying alimony has no effect on the obligation, even if the remarriage results in less available income for the paying spouse due to needs of the new spouse or step-children. These are considered voluntary obligations and cannot replace the existing alimony obligation. In some cases, however, if the paying spouse has children with the former spouse and additional children, either through birth or legal adoption, with the new spouse, there might be an impact on total support due to a recalculation of child support. You can get a better understanding of how this might happen by reviewing the New Jersey Child Support Guidelines.

The remarriage of a supported spouse, on the other hand, is an event that ordinarily triggers automatic termination of alimony. Each member of a married couple has a mutual obligation to support the other, both emotionally and financially, and alimony represents the limited continuation of the financial part of this obligation for equitable reasons. Once a spouse receiving alimony has entered into a legal relationship entailing mutual obligations of support with a new spouse, the former spouse is released. The only thing that might prevent this would be a separation agreement between the couple that very clearly provides for continuing alimony even in the event of remarriage. In the usual case, however, the obligation is permanently terminated, and even if the new marriage fails, alimony will not be reinstated. A spouse who enters into a new marriage while receiving a significant amount of alimony after a previous long-term marriage must take this into consideration in planning for the future.

Cohabitation

The cohabitation of an alimony recipient with a new romantic partner can be a ground for modification, suspension, or termination of alimony payments. Different states evaluate this type of situation according to varying criteria. In New Jersey, the fact of cohabitation alone is not enough to justify a reduction in payments. There must also be economic consequences supporting the modification. The main reason courts will often reduce alimony in this type of situation is to prevent an abuse of one of the main purposes of alimony, which is to provide financial support to a dependent spouse who has lost the support of the former marriage partner. If the new couple is acting as a married couple, and the supported spouse is now receiving economic benefits from participating in the new partnership, it would be unfair to the spouse paying alimony to require a continuation of support simply because the new couple is choosing to remain technically unmarried.

A court assessing the impact of cohabitation will first consider whether or not the cohabitation is sufficiently similar to a marriage to justify treating it in a similar manner. If it is, and the supported spouse's new romantic partner is contributing to household expenses and thus reducing the financial needs of the supported spouse, a reduction may be appropriate. If the new partner is not contributing to household expenses but the supported spouse is instead paying expenses for the new partner, a court may also order a reduction. A former spouse paying alimony clearly has no obligation to subsidize the financial needs of an ex-spouse's new partner.

The paying spouse must demonstrate evidence of cohabitation. The 2014 statutory amendments make clear, however, that it is not necessary for parties to live together full time to have a "cohabiting" relationship, specifically stating that cohabitation does not require maintenance of a single common household. This is an important feature from an evidentiary perspective; it means that an obligor no longer needs to hire a private investigator to stake out a home for days on end just to verify that a recipient's new partner is in permanent residence. While sharing a permanent residence is still an important factor, it is not a necessary one; a litigant can prove cohabitation through application of the following listed factors:

- Intertwined finances such as joint bank accounts and other joint holdings or liabilities;

- Sharing or joint responsibility for living expenses;

- Recognition of the relationship in the couple's social and family circle;

- Living together, the frequency of contact, the duration of the relationship, and other indicia of a mutually supportive intimate personal relationship;

- Sharing household chores;

- Whether the recipient of alimony has received an enforceable promise of support from another person within the meaning of subsection h. of R.S.25:1-5; and

All other relevant evidence.
N.J.S.A. 2A:34-23n.

The duration of a cohabitation relationship is especially important. An essential feature is that a relationship must be serious and enduring before it can be the basis for an alimony modification. While no minimum length is specified in the statute, the cohabitation would probably have to last for at least several months before a court would seriously consider it to be "enduring." Courts have tended to require a fairly high level of proof on this point, to avoid interfering with the right of a single person to enter into simple dating relationships, regardless of economic need or receipt of alimony. Courts also recognize that cohabitation relationships, by legal definition, are not subject to the mutual obligations of spousal support created by a legal marriage, are more easily ended than marriages, and therefore may be inherently less stable than marriages, particularly in the early stages. Allowing courts discretion to suspend alimony rather than terminate it permanently takes this aspect into account.

If a judge finds sufficient evidence of cohabitation, limited discovery and a hearing may be conducted to determine whether the cohabitation gives rise to a change of economic circumstances. The alimony recipient can then present evidence attempting to show that there is no economic consequence deriving from the cohabitation.

Requesting an Increase in Payments

An alimony recipient can generally request an increase for the same kinds of reasons that would justify a decrease. For example, a recipient who has been laid off from a job due to a work slowdown can request an increase in alimony if the lay-off is permanent and the spouse cannot find a comparable new position. A spouse who was expecting to be fully employed within a brief period of time and has not been successful in finding employment may also have a claim. In either case, the claim will require the same type of documentation as a claim requesting a decrease in payment due to job loss, including proof that the applicant is doing everything possible to become fully employed. Required documentation will include an updated CIS, recent tax returns, W-2's or evidence of self-employment income, an updated resume, and a detailed log demonstrating efforts to find work.

A motion for an increase could also be based on increased costs of living due to various factors. Whatever the increased costs may be, documentary proof will be required. A judge considering a motion for an increase will consider both the recipient's increased need and the payer's ability to pay an additional amount. Only in a very unusual case would a court be likely to order an increase that would result in the paying spouse living significantly below the marital standard of living. A court also will not order an increase that would result in the recipient's standard of living improving beyond that enjoyed during the marriage. If your former spouse wins the lottery and becomes a billionaire, you may be able to get an increase if your initial award left you with a shortfall, but beyond this, you are not likely to have a good argument entitling you to share in the post-marital wealth.

Chapter 7

Alimony Case Studies

Alimony calculations typically involve consideration of many factors. In trying to get even a "ballpark" estimate of what might happen in your case, be very careful not to rely on any other cases, even a case that appears very similar to your own.

The following are fairly typical examples. They are a combination or real and hypothetical scenarios. In studies that chronicle real events, all of the parties' names have been changed to protect the privacy of the families. In each case, we explain how the situation was resolved under the pre-reform statute, and what the major differences would be under the revised statute. We have also noted how changes in the federal tax code might affect these cases if alimony was ordered or agreed upon in 2019 or later.

1) Long-Term Marriage with Stay-at-Home Mother
2) High Earning Wife
3) Shorter Marriage without Children
4) Intermediate Length Marriage with Two Working Parents
5) Alimony Modification Denied Due to No Current Change in Circumstances
6) Alimony Termination Granted Pursuant to Terms of Marital Settlement Agreement Regarding Cohabitation
7) Alimony Modification Granted to Reflect the Intent of the Parties in their Marital Settlement Agreement
8) Modification of Alimony and Child Support Denied Due to Voluntary Nature of Unemployment

1. Long-Term Marriage with Stay-at-Home Mother

Lisa and Chris were married for 18 years. At the time of the divorce complaint both were in good health; Lisa was 48 years old and Chris was 52. They had three children, ages 16, 13, and 10. Lisa graduated from college but was a full-time stay-at-home parent for the last 16 years. Chris earned $180,000 annually, and also typically received an annual bonus. The bonus was not guaranteed, but it averaged $25,000 per year for the past three years.

Lisa and Chris were not able to reach agreement regarding an appropriate amount of alimony, and their case ended up in court. The court ordered Chris to pay Lisa permanent alimony in the base amount of $50,000 per year, plus 28% of Chris's future bonuses, all taxable to Lisa as income and tax deductible for Chris. As part of the calculation, the court determined that since the children were now all in school full-time, Lisa would be able to return to the work force in the immediate future and earn $25,000 per year.

This case was decided prior to the revisions to the alimony statute that changed permanent alimony to open durational alimony. This means that if Chris wants to reduce or terminate his alimony payments when he retires, he will have to bring a motion in court. If he has reached age 66 (his full retirement age under the Social Security Act), the court will begin with a presumption that his retirement is in good faith, but he will retain the burden of proving that modification or termination is appropriate under the N.J.S.A 2A:34-23j(3) factors.

Because Lisa and Chris were married for fewer than 20 years, if this case were to be decided under the revised statute, Lisa would not receive an open durational award unless she was able to demonstrate exceptional circumstances. She could, however, receive an award with a term of up to 18 years (the length of the marriage). Either way, after 14 years, the award would terminate unless she was able to demonstrate that it should not, because Chris would then be 66 years old, and therefore entitled to the presumption favoring termination at full retirement age for orders instituted under the new statute.

If this case was decided in 2019 or later, both the base amount of alimony and the percentage of bonuses awarded to Lisa would undoubtedly be significantly lower, as Chris would be responsible for paying taxes on the alimony payments and Lisa would not.

2. High-Earning Wife

Alimony is no longer just for women! As this case demonstrates, it is not out of the ordinary in this day and age for a wife to earn substantially more than her husband. If a husband asks a wife to pay alimony, a court will not hesitate to apply the same factors that courts have traditionally examined when awarding alimony to a wife:

Kathleen and Ryan were married for 12 years. At the time of their divorce Kathleen was 40 years old and Ryan was 42; both were in good health. They had two children together, Jessica, who was six years old and in the first grade, and Jenna, who was two and was attending day care each morning from 9:30 am to 12:30 pm.

Ryan drove the children to and from school and day care and watched both of them in the afternoons. He worked part-time from home, earning approximately $30,000 per year. Kathleen had a demanding full-time job involving a considerable amount of both domestic and international travel. She was typically away from home for a quarter to half of the nights during each month. Kathleen was earning almost $350,000 per year.

The court awarded Ryan limited duration alimony in the amount of $100,000 per year for a period of eight years after a thorough analysis of all of the alimony statutory factors.

The result in this case would likely be very similar, regardless of whether it was decided before or after the 2014 alimony reforms. Because Ryan and Kathleen were married for 12 years, the maximum duration of alimony would now be 12 years, unless Ryan could demonstrate extraordinary circumstances.

If this case was decided in 2019 or later, the amount of the alimony award would probably be somewhat lower, to account for the fact that Kathleen would be responsible for paying taxes on the payments and Ryan would not.

3. Shorter Marriage without Children

The following case demonstrates that alimony is not always necessary or appropriate, particularly after a shorter marriage where the parties have relatively equal earning power and no children:

Betsy and Rick were married for six years and had no children together. At the time of their divorce, Betsy was 33 years old and Rick was 32. Both of them were in good health and both were college graduates. Rick had recently earned his MBA, and had considerable student debt as a result. The student loans were in his name only and he would be solely responsible for them after the divorce. Rick was earning approximately $110,000 per year, while Betsy earned $95,000 per year. The court determined that Betsy and Rick were both self-supporting and there was no alimony ordered in this case.

Neither the 2014 statutory revisions nor the tax changes of 2019 would have any significant impact on this outcome.

4. Intermediate Length Marriage with Two Working Parents

The following case demonstrates how a court might calculate alimony after an intermediate-term marriage where both spouses have been continuously employed but there is a significant income discrepancy:

Amy and Grant were married for eight years. When they decided to divorce, Amy was 32 years old and Grant was 39. Both were college-educated, in good health, and employed full-time. They had one child who was five years old and attending kindergarten. Amy earned $45,000 per year and Grant earned $75,000 per year.

In this case the court ordered Grant to pay Amy the amount of $10,000 per year in limited duration alimony (taxable to Amy as income and tax-deductible for Grant), for a period of four years.

Under the reformed statute, a similar result could be anticipated. The maximum term for alimony after this marriage would be eight years, absent a showing of exceptional circumstances.

If the case were decided in 2019 or later, the alimony would no longer be taxable to Amy or tax-deductible for Grant. The amount awarded would probably be slightly lower, although the tax effects would be less significant at this level that at the level of the higher award amounts discussed above.

5. Alimony Modification Denied Due to No Current Change in Circumstances

The following case demonstrates how courts handled modifications based on loss of income prior to the 2014 alimony reforms, and how this would now be different post-reform:

Carol and John were married for 22 years and had been divorced for six years when John sought a modification of his alimony obligation. At the time of the divorce, John was earning $200,000 per year and Carol was not employed. John and Carol entered into a settlement agreement according to which John was to pay Carol permanent alimony in the amount of $60,000 per year.

John learned that his company was downsizing and that his position would soon be eliminated. He would be receiving a two-month severance package. He applied to the court requesting a downward modification of his alimony obligation in light of this situation. Unfortunately for John, the court denied his application as premature.

The court stated that even though John had in fact experienced a change in circumstance due to his job loss, he failed to demonstrate to the court that the change would necessarily affect his income on a long-term basis. Before the court would allow John to reduce his alimony obligation, he would have to show that a considerable amount of time had elapsed following the job loss, and that during this lapse of time he had diligently applied for comparable jobs.

At the time John filed his motion, he was still within the two-month severance period, and so he had not yet experienced any drop in income. The court ordered him to continue making alimony payments to Carol with no adjustment.

Under the revised statute, John would have been aware that he needed to wait a minimum of 90 days following his job loss before applying for modification on that basis. The court would still require evidence that he had been diligently applying for work during the 90-day period.

6. Alimony Termination Granted Pursuant to Terms of Marital Settlement Agreement Regarding Cohabitation

The following case illustrates several important aspects of alimony and settlement agreements. First, it shows how a former spouse who is paying alimony might make use of a private investigator to prove that the alimony recipient is involved in a marriage-like relationship with a new partner. Second, it demonstrates the impact of specifying terms regarding cohabitation and alimony modification in a marital settlement agreement. Third, it shows how important it can be to file a modification motion as soon as it becomes clear that circumstances have substantially changed, because changes in payment obligations will generally be effective as of the date the motion is filed, even if it takes the court several months to make a final decision on the motion. Finally, it shows how cohabitation was treated prior to September of 2014 as opposed to how it has been treated since that date:

Kurt and Sarah were divorced after 14 years of marriage. At the time of the divorce, Kurt was earning $85,000 per year. Although Sarah had not worked during the marriage and was not employed at the time of the divorce, the couple agreed that she had the ability to earn $25,000 per year.

Kurt and Sarah entered into a marital settlement agreement requiring Kurt to pay Sarah limited duration alimony in the amount of $15,000 per year for ten years. The agreement also specifically stated that if Sarah was to cohabit with an unrelated adult in a relationship tantamount to marriage, Kurt could seek court intervention requesting a reduction or termination of his alimony payment obligation.

About four years after the divorce, Kurt became aware that Sarah's long-term boyfriend had been spending a lot of time at her home. She denied that the boyfriend had moved in with her, but Kurt did not believe she was being truthful. Friends who knew both Kurt and Sarah confirmed that he was right to be suspicious, because the boyfriend was in fact officially living at Sarah's home.

Kurt decided to hire a private investigator to conduct surveillance. The investigator videotaped the boyfriend entering Sarah's home both with his own key and via the garage with an opener that he kept in his car. The tape also showed him carrying groceries into the home, working on the yard, retrieving mail from the mailbox, and greeting neighbors in the driveway. A witness verified that the boyfriend had forwarded his mail to Sarah's address, that he often invited friends to the home, and that he had recently participated in a holiday party at the home which included members of both Sarah's family and his own family.

Kurt filed a motion in court requesting a modification of his alimony obligation based on the fact that Sarah was in a new relationship that was tantamount to marriage. The court held a plenary hearing and examined all of the evidence, including witness testimony and the surveillance tape created by the private investigator. Following the hearing, the judge ordered Kurt's alimony obligation terminated as of the date that he had originally filed his motion with the court. Sarah was ordered to reimburse Kurt for alimony payments he made to her between the date he filed his motion and the date of the court's decision.

Because the rules regarding alimony and cohabitation with new romantic partners had not yet been codified by statute, Kurt and Sarah were wise to outline the specifics of the impact of cohabitation in their separation agreement.

Under the revised statute, however, cohabitation would have been somewhat easier to prove. While the investigator's tape would still be very helpful, it would have been less necessary, because the revised statute does not require proof that a new partner is living permanently at the alimony recipient's address.

7. Alimony Modification Granted to Reflect the Intent of the Parties in their Marital Settlement Agreement

Weinberger Divorce & Family Law Group represented the former wife, Olivia, in this post-judgment matter involving modification of alimony payments under a marital settlement agreement. Olivia was represented by a different attorney at the time of her divorce:

Olivia and Harold were married for nine years. Harold was the breadwinner throughout the marriage while Olivia did not work outside the home. During the last three years of the marriage, Harold's income averaged over $100,000 per year.

At the time of the divorce, Olivia was studying for her real estate license. Both she and Harold believed that she would soon be able to get a job selling real estate and would consequently be able to support herself within just a few years. Olivia and Harold entered into a marital settlement agreement requiring Harold to pay Olivia rehabilitative alimony for two years.

Soon after Olivia and Harold finalized their divorce, there was a sudden and substantial downturn in the economy, resulting in a severe and long-lasting impact on the real estate market. Although Olivia succeeded in obtaining her real estate license, she was unable to find a job with a base salary. She was forced to rely on commission-only jobs during a time when even the most skillful and experienced real estate agents were having difficulty completing any sales. Consequently, Olivia was not able to earn enough to become self-supporting.

Two months before the date that alimony payments were scheduled to end under the marital settlement agreement, Olivia retained counsel to attempt to extend the alimony term. Her attorney filed a motion requesting an extension of Harold's alimony obligation based on Olivia's continuing need for spousal support and her inability, despite diligent efforts, to become self-supporting.

The court found that both parties had intended the temporary alimony payments to be rehabilitative, with the purpose of assisting Olivia in getting back on her feet after the divorce. The court also found that Harold was still able to pay the alimony. Although he claimed that his income had significantly diminished since the divorce, the court noted that he regularly went to Atlantic City on the weekends to gamble and had won tens of thousands of dollars this way. The court extended Harold's obligation to make alimony payments to Olivia for an additional three-year term.

The 2014 alimony revisions would have no significant impact on this case.

8. Modification of Alimony and Child Support Denied Due to Voluntary Nature of Unemployment

This case demonstrates that unemployment is not a change in circumstances that will justify a modification of a support obligation if the unemployment is essentially voluntary:

Weinberger Divorce & Family Law Group represented the former wife, Jennifer, in the combined child support and alimony case. Jennifer and Jason had been married for 24 years and had three children together. Jason was the primary breadwinner throughout the marriage and at the time of the divorce, Jennifer had not worked in almost 20 years. The court ordered Jason to pay child support and permanent alimony to Jennifer.

Approximately one year after the divorce, Jason filed a motion for modification of his support obligations based on the fact that he had decided to accept a severance package from his employer and was no longer working. Jason claimed that he had made this decision on the basis that he suffered from a form of arthritis that prevented him from continuing in his current job. Jennifer's attorney filed an opposition to Jason's motion arguing that he had not provided any medical documentation of his alleged disability and had not applied for Social Security disability benefits. He also had not demonstrated that he was unable to continue any kind of gainful employment and had failed to provide documentation showing a good faith attempt to obtain another job.

The court found that Jason's unemployment was voluntarily and that he was therefore unable to establish the substantial change in circumstances required for a modification of his support obligations. The court denied his motion and ordered him to continue paying alimony and child support in the original amounts.

The 2014 revisions to the alimony statute would not significantly impact this case.

Further Information and Resources

- Weinberger Divorce & Family Law Group provides detailed information on its website about alimony, including a discussion of types of alimony and statutory factors, located at: http://bit.ly/spousal-support

- For additional information about New Jersey "palimony," please refer to the Weinberger Divorce & Family Law Group website: http://bit.ly/palimony.

- Alimony is not just for women. As women achieve more and more success in the workforce, alimony payments from former wives to former husbands are on the rise. For a summary of a CBS2 report on "manimony," featuring attorney Bari Z. Weinberger, please visit http://bit.ly/manimony.

- For a look at the historical development at alimony reform in New Jersey, see "Status of Alimony Reform in New Jersey" at: http://bit.ly/alimony-reform.

For More Information

At Weinberger Divorce & Family Law Group all of our attorneys are engaged full time in the practice of family law. We are committed to providing honest recommendations and keeping the best interests of our clients and their children at the forefront at all times. Our attorneys will strive to resolve your matter out of court and will explore your settlement options, including New Jersey divorce mediation if appropriate in your case. When necessary, we will also fight vigorously to protect your rights.

You can find out more about our dedicated family law attorneys on our website, which is located at: WeinbergerLawGroup.com. Weinberger Divorce & Family Law Group offers an initial consultation with an experienced New Jersey Family Law Attorney at no cost.

Weinberger Divorce & Family Law Group has several offices located throughout New Jersey.

Weinberger Divorce & Family Law Group Headquarter Offices:

119 Cherry Hill Road, Suite 120
Parsippany, NJ 07054
Morris County

Tel: (888) 888-0919

Weinberger Divorce
& Family Law Group
Safeguarding Your Future™

Other Book Titles: Weinberger Law Group Library Series of Family Law Guides

Contested Divorce

Uncontested Divorce

Child Support

Child Custody

Property Division

Relationship Agreements

Alternative Dispute Resolution

Print books and ebook versions of the Weinberger Law Group Library series can be ordered via Amazon or by visiting www.WeinbergerLawGroup.com.

Printed in Dunstable, United Kingdom

91233272R00067